YES, I SPY!
I SPY ... ANIMALS

© Smart Little Owl

I spy with my little eye, something beginning with...

A is for alligator!

I spy with my little eye, something beginning with...

B

B

is for
bee!

I spy with my little eye, something beginning with...

C

is for
crab!

I spy with my little eye, something beginning with...

D and E

D is for dolphin!

E is for elephant!

I spy with my little eye, something beginning with...

F

F
is for
fox!

I spy with my little eye, something beginning with...

G and H

G

is for
giraffe!

H

is for
hedgehog!

I spy with my little eye, something beginning with...

I is for iguana!

I spy with my little eye, something beginning with...

J and K

J
is for
jellyfish!

K
is for
kangaroo!

I spy with my little eye, something beginning with...

L

is for
lion!

I spy with my little eye, something beginning with...

M and N

M

is for
moose!

N

is for
nightingale!

I spy with my little eye, something beginning with...

O

O is for owl!

I spy with my little eye, something beginning with...

P is for parrot!

I spy with my little eye, something beginning with...

Q and R

Q is for
quail!

R is for
raccoon!

I spy with my little eye, something beginning with...

S is for snake!

I spy with my little eye, something beginning with...

T and U

T is for turtle!

U is for unicorn!

I spy with my little eye, something beginning with...

V is for vulture!

I spy with my little eye, something beginning with...

W is for walrus!

I spy with my little eye, something beginning with...

X is for x-ray fish!

I spy with my little eye, something beginning with...

Y is for yak!

I spy with my little eye, something beginning with...

Z

is for
zebra!

More Books From Smart Little Owl

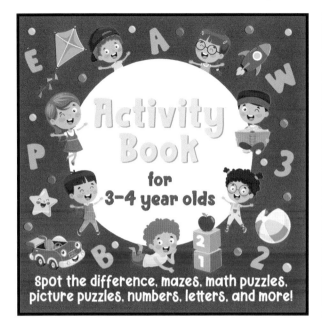

Activity Book for 3-4 year olds

spot the difference, mazes, math puzzles, picture puzzles, numbers, letters, and more!

YES, I SPY! I SPY ... EVERYTHING

Tracing Numbers from 1 to 10

Beginner math preschool learning book with number tracing and coloring activities for preschoolers

Prewriting Skills Workbook for toddlers

Fun pen control and tracing for 3 year olds

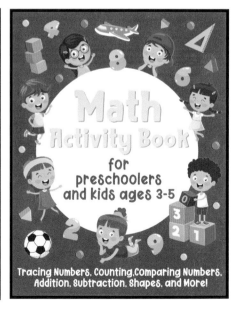

Math Activity Book for preschoolers and kids ages 3-5

Tracing Numbers, Counting, Comparing Numbers, Addition, Subtraction, Shapes, and More!

Printed in Great Britain
by Amazon